SAXMUNDHAM TO YARMOUTH

**Richard Adderson and
Graham Kenworthy**

MP Middleton Press

Cover picture: A scruffy class K3 2-6-0, no. 61981, heads an up express at Beccles during the late 1950s. These mixed traffic engines proved a godsend to hard-pressed shedmasters, and were often to be found on express passenger trains, especially on Summer Saturdays. (H.N.James/J.Day)

First published September 2001
Reprinted May 2004

ISBN 1 901706 69 9

© *Middleton Press, 2001*

Design - Deborah Esher

Published by

    Middleton Press
    Easebourne Lane
    Midhurst, West Sussex
    GU29 9AZ
Tel: 01730 813169
Fax: 01730 812601
info@middletonpress.co.uk
www.middletonpress.co.uk

Printed & bound by
    MPG Books, Bodmin, Cornwall

INDEX

ACKNOWLEDGEMENTS

In addition to the photographers acknowledged in the photographic credits, we are most grateful to the following people for their assistance in the compilation of this book; K.Buttifant, E.Dove, J.Richardson, and F.Tanner.

Readers of this book may be interested to know of the Great Eastern Railway Society. The membership secretary is -

J.R.Tant
9 Clare Road
Leytonstone
London E11 1JU

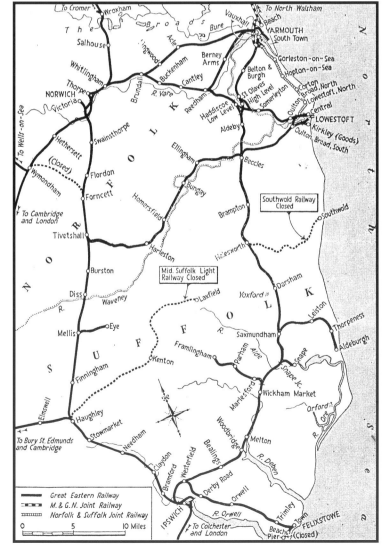

I. Railways of the area in 1954. The pre-1923 ownerships are shown, but not all the stations on the minor lines are marked (Railway Magazine). Other maps in this volume are to a scale of 25 ins to 1 mile, unless otherwise stated.

GEOGRAPHICAL SETTING

The northern end of the East Suffolk Line continues from Saxmundham in much the same way as the southern end, as a coastal railway, but about six to eight miles or so inland. At Beccles, however, the present line turns sharply eastwards and makes a bee-line for the coast at Lowestoft, along what was originally a branch line. Prior to the closure north of Beccles in 1959, the main line's objective was also the seaside, but further north, at Great Yarmouth.

The theme of the railway following the contours of an undulating countryside also continues, resulting in a saw-toothed gradient profile and many curves as the line heads almost due north from Saxmundham, negotiating a further series of broadly east-west river valleys. Beyond Beccles the nature of the line changed, most of the land on this final section being less than 50 feet above sea level.

Saxmundham is almost exactly 91 miles from London, and the line immediately begins a sharp two mile climb past the Aldeburgh branch junction, before an equally sharp two mile descent to cross the Minsmere River just before Darsham. A similar pattern follows as the line climbs and then falls to cross the River Blyth on the southern approach to Halesworth at the 100 mile post. Yet again, a steep two mile ascent takes the line on to something of a plateau, but with undulations,

before the final 1 in 87 plunge into the valley of the River Waveney at Beccles, which stands just beyond the 109 mile post and is almost at sea level.

From here the route to Yarmouth had to overcome two areas of only slightly higher ground around Aldeby and Belton; but, more significantly, the meandering, but navigable, River Waveney had to be crossed twice before the terminus was reached at just under 122 miles from Liverpool Street. Both of these river crossings were accomplished via swing bridges.

Between the sites of these bridges, the River Waveney marks the Suffolk / Norfolk county boundary, involving the route in a short incursion into the latter county. At the time of the opening, the remainder of the line from St Olaves Swing Bridge was wholly in Suffolk, but a change in the municipal boundary in 1891 meant that the final ¾ mile or so into Yarmouth South Town was transferred to Norfolk.

The name "Great Yarmouth", although in common use before the coming of the railway, was never adopted by the railway authorities; in fact, the parish of South Town was commonly referred to as "Little Yarmouth", a name that was hardly in keeping with the railway's aspirations.

This gradient diagram dates from the LNER period. However, as a result of later surveys, the gradients may be slightly different from those shown on gradient posts in more recent times.

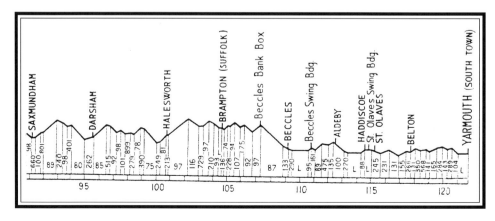

HISTORICAL BACKGROUND

As mentioned in the volume covering Ipswich to Saxmundham, the north-east corner of the county of Suffolk had been left unconnected to the fast growing national network by the failure of a number of schemes proposed in the Railway Mania years of the late 1840s.

However, Samuel Morton Peto, who had achieved his primary aim in 1847 of linking Lowestoft with Norwich, and therefore with London, decided that a rather simpler scheme benefitting Beccles and Halesworth might succeed. This new approach led to the successful promotion of a line heading north into Norfolk, the Halesworth, Beccles & Haddiscoe Railway. The line would connect at Haddiscoe with the 1847 line mentioned above; the Act was passed in 1851, and the line opened to passengers on 4th December 1854.

This success led to renewed efforts to complete the route southwards from Halesworth towards Ipswich, as well as extending northwards from Haddiscoe to Yarmouth. The first step was achieved in 1854; when an Act authorising the section from Halesworth to Woodbridge (and the change of name to the East Suffolk Railway) was passed. At Woodbridge it would make an end-on junction with a line constructed under renewed powers first granted to the Eastern Union Railway in 1847. The final piece of the jigsaw was authorised by the Yarmouth and Haddiscoe Act of 1856.

The original single line section from Haddiscoe to Halesworth was closed from 17th May 1858 for what was expected to be two to three months, to enable it to be relaid to double track standards. In the event, a lack of will from the Eastern Union, together with some engineering problems on their stretch of line, delayed the re-opening for over a year. The East Suffolk line was opened throughout, on 1st June, 1859, under Eastern Counties Railway operation.

Meanwhile, various leases and mergers had taken place, and these led ultimately to the formation of the Great Eastern Railway by Act of Parliament on 7th August 1862, by amalgamation of the Eastern Counties, the Eastern Union, the Norfolk, the East Suffolk and the East Anglian Railways.

The Great Eastern Railway passed into the ownership of the London & North Eastern Railway on 1st January 1923, and the lines became part of the Eastern Region of British Railways upon Nationalisation on 1st January 1948. During the 86 year period of GER and LNER ownership there were few major developments, apart from the gradual introduction of interlocking to the signalling system.

Although newspaper reports of possible closure of the section between Beccles and Yarmouth South Town began to appear as early as 1955, the section survived as a through route until 2nd November 1959, all services after that date being diverted via the former branch line to Lowestoft and thence over the former Norfolk and Suffolk Joint Line via Gorleston. The main reason given by British Railways for closure was the disproportionately high cost of maintaining the swing bridges at Beccles and St Olaves. This decision resulted in the Beccles to Oulton Broad branch being, effectively, elevated to main line status. Final services should have run on Sunday 13th September, but, due to a printers' strike, production of winter timetables was disrupted, resulting in a seven week reprieve.

The infamous Beeching Report of March 1963 proposed the closure to passengers of the whole of the East Suffolk line. In the event the through route was reprieved by the Minister of Transport in 1966, although by then Darsham, Halesworth and Brampton had been closed to freight; Beccles continued to handle a dwindling amount of goods traffic until early 1968.

All stations became unstaffed halts when on-train issuing of tickets commenced on 6th March 1967, almost four months after the introduction, on 11th November 1966, of the revised services which had been planned in connection with conductor-guard working. The northernmost end of the original line, the last ½ mile into Yarmouth South Town Station, continued to be served from Lowestoft until closure on 4th May 1970.

In 1984 preparatory work began on rationalisation of the route and the automation of all level crossings, culminating in the introduction of Radio Electronic Tokenless Block (RETB) on 16th February 1986. The line was singled between Halesworth and Oulton Broad North Junction and conventional signalling abolished, all train movements being controlled and monitored from the adapted signalbox at Saxmundham.

Since introduction of RETB working, there has been no regular freight traffic between Saxmundham Junction and Lowestoft.

Following Privatisation on 5th January 1997, the remaining passenger services were operated by Anglia Railways.

PASSENGER SERVICES

Having provided an indication of the basic winter services on the line in "Ipswich to Saxmundham", it was felt that a balance should struck by indicating the level of summer services when dealing with the second volume. But, once again, it is only possible to show those trains which ran each weekday. Details of stops at St Olaves Junction (subsequently re-named Herringfleet Junction and Haddiscoe High Level) Exchange Station have been omitted completely in the interests of clarity.

The weekday service provided on the opening of the first section of the line in 1854 comprised three trains each way, leaving Halesworth at 9.00 am, 11.45 am and 4.00 pm, and returning from Haddiscoe at 10.18 am, 1.55 pm and 5.10 pm.

When the East Suffolk line opened throughout, the first timetable, that for 1st June 1859, showed four trains in each direction between Ipswich and Yarmouth. In the down direction three of these called at all stations, leaving Saxmundham at 8.00 am, 1.10 pm and 7.52 pm, while the 3.26 pm called only at Saxmundham, Halesworth and Beccles. Of the four up trains from Yarmouth, two, the 10.45 am and 3.30 pm, made the same calls, and only two were "all stations", leaving the northern terminus at 5.30 am and 5.45 pm.

Exactly thirteen years after the opening of the main line, a new spur between Marsh Junction (on the Reedham to Lowestoft line) and St Olaves Swing Bridge Junction was opened. This enabled a direct service to be run from Lowestoft to Yarmouth South Town and, as a consequence, the northern extremity of the line received something of a boost in services. The first timetable, that for June 1872, showed that seven trains were provided in each direction, although stops were only made at St Olaves and Belton "when required".

By July, 1883 there were eight down trains between Saxmundham and Yarmouth, four of which called at all stations; the remainder had a variety of stopping patterns and included two which called only at Beccles. Of the eight, six originated from Liverpool Street. There was an additional express service from London, which called only at Beccles on the run from Ipswich to Yarmouth. Two short, "all stations" workings between Beccles and Yarmouth plus the, by now, five "direct" trains from Lowestoft, still serving

St Olaves and Belton "when required", completed the picture. Up services followed a broadly similar pattern, but are not detailed.

The increased demand for travel in the late Victorian / early Edwardian era meant that, by the time of the summer timetable for 1909, ten trains, all originating from Liverpool Street, provided the weekday service from Saxmundham northwards. Five of these called "all stations" (although one declined the opportunity of serving Aldeby). As in 1883, there was also an express which called only at Beccles on the East Suffolk Line. Perhaps of more significance than the general increase in services was the fact that there was a daily "Yarmouth and Gorleston Express" which left Liverpool Street at 10.20 am and ran non-stop to Yarmouth. The "all stations" local workings north of Beccles had increased to three, while the "direct" services originating at Lowestoft were at the same level as they had been twenty-six years earlier.

The inexorable rise in services to satisfy the requirements of an increasingly holiday-minded public stalled briefly during, and immediately after, World War I, but by the summer of 1938 the popularity of train travel and of the Yarmouth area as a holiday destination led to the provision of no less 14 trains between Saxmundham and Yarmouth, nine of them starting from London. By this date, a number of weekday trains ran to slightly different times and with slightly different stopping patterns on Saturdays; in this summary these trains have been included if there is an obviously close correlation. Of the total, six called at all stations, the remainder making intermediate stops at Halesworth and Beccles, or at Beccles only. In addition there were five "all station shuttles" between Beccles and Yarmouth. The Lowestoft to Yarmouth "direct" service, calling at St Olaves and Belton had been withdrawn in 1934; in the summer of 1929 it had comprised seven return trips, six of which were operated by a steam railmotor.

In the post World War II years the increase in Saturday-to-Saturday family holidays on the coast between Lowestoft and Yarmouth was sufficient to justify the splitting of "Weekday" train services, and pages in the summer timetable, into "Mondays to Fridays" and "Saturdays Only" categories. The 1959 edition, commencing on 15th June, was the final one to cover the section north of Beccles.

On Mondays to Fridays, 15 out of 21 northbound departures from Saxmundham to Beccles were operated by DMUs, all but one of the six which were destined for Yarmouth calling at all stations; the remaining nine were services to Lowestoft, most of them only stopping at Halesworth. The six DMUs north of Beccles were augmented by a further five originating there, and of the eleven, all but the last one (9.20 pm ex-Beccles) called at all stations. There were six loco-hauled trains between Saxmundham and Yarmouth, each shedding a Lowestoft portion at Beccles. The first originated at Ipswich and called at all stations; the second started from Colchester, and, in common with the remainder, which were through expresses from London, called only at Halesworth and Beccles.

The only other weekday service on the line was a 6.47 am departure from Halesworth to Lowestoft, which on Mondays to Fridays failed to connect with the first Beccles to Yarmouth train by four minutes. All was well on Saturdays, however, as the Yarmouth train left Beccles ten minutes later.

The rest of the Saturday services bore little resemblance to those of Monday to Friday; DMUs were almost completely absent and there were only 16 trains, with a variety of stopping patterns, between Saxmundham and Beccles as against 21 on the other five days. Of the 16, 12 formed onward services to Yarmouth, 11 of them serving all stations, while the final train of the day ran non-stop. Preparations for closure had obviously been made as 15 trains from London (i.e. the remaining 4 trains from Saxmundham, plus 11 others which were non-stop from Ipswich to Beccles) ran to Lowestoft, before completing the onward journey to South Town via Gorleston.

By Summer 1979 only Saxmundham to Beccles of the original line survived. The remaining through daily service to and from London (07.22 from Lowestoft and 16.50 from Liverpool Street) called at all stations except Brampton in both directions; it ran for the last time on 12th May 1984. Nine down trains on the Ipswich to Lowestoft DMU service plus an early morning train northwards from Halesworth, called at all stations. The up service was similar, except that the first train of the morning omitted a Brampton stop.

A through London service was reintroduced in the Summer of 1999; the timetable for 2000 showed this train calling at all stations in both directions. All stations were also served by all other services, amounting to nine in the down direction and eight in the up.

December 1938 timetable.

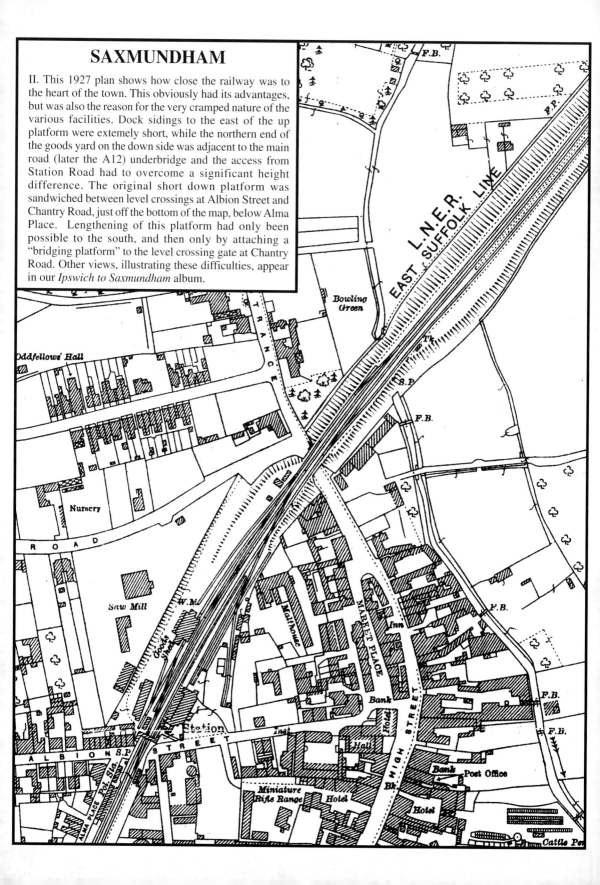

SAXMUNDHAM

II. This 1927 plan shows how close the railway was to the heart of the town. This obviously had its advantages, but was also the reason for the very cramped nature of the various facilities. Dock sidings to the east of the up platform were extemely short, while the northern end of the goods yard on the down side was adjacent to the main road (later the A12) underbridge and the access from Station Road had to overcome a significant height difference. The original short down platform was sandwiched between level crossings at Albion Street and Chantry Road, just off the bottom of the map, below Alma Place. Lengthening of this platform had only been possible to the south, and then only by attaching a "bridging platform" to the level crossing gate at Chantry Road. Other views, illustrating these difficulties, appear in our *Ipswich to Saxmundham* album.

1.   We start our journey on a lazy September afternoon in 1956. Not much is happening, as we look north from the station footbridge along the sweeping S bend of the main line. The bookstall has closed for the day, but a few passengers are enjoying the sunshine on the up platform as they wait for their train to arrive. In the middle distance a rake of wagons is parked on the steeply graded "Hay siding", and beyond them we can just make out the junction signal box and the embankment of the Aldeburgh branch. The roof of the signal box featured in the following photograph appears in the bottom left hand corner. (Photomatic)

2.   Representing the new generation of through London trains, no. 170207 runs into the down platform on 9th September 2000 as the 16.27 from Liverpool Street to Lowestoft. This platform had been built on the site of the former goods yard some twenty years earlier. The signal box, since 1986 the control centre for the RETB system, formerly contained a frame of 43 levers. (R.J.Adderson)

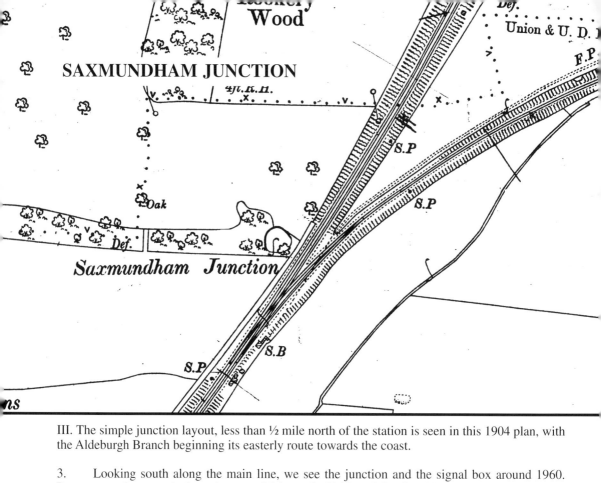

III. The simple junction layout, less than ½ mile north of the station is seen in this 1904 plan, with the Aldeburgh Branch beginning its easterly route towards the coast.

3.   Looking south along the main line, we see the junction and the signal box around 1960. Passenger trains over the branch were withdrawn in 1966, and the signal box was demolished soon afterwards. However, an occasional freight train serving the power station at Sizewell ensured that much of the branch survived into the 21st century. (NRS Archive)

DARSHAM

IV. Expansion of rail facilities at this location had just about reached its peak by the time of this 1904 plan. The main road, which later became the A12, however, has continued its relentless progress towards a similar status for almost a century.

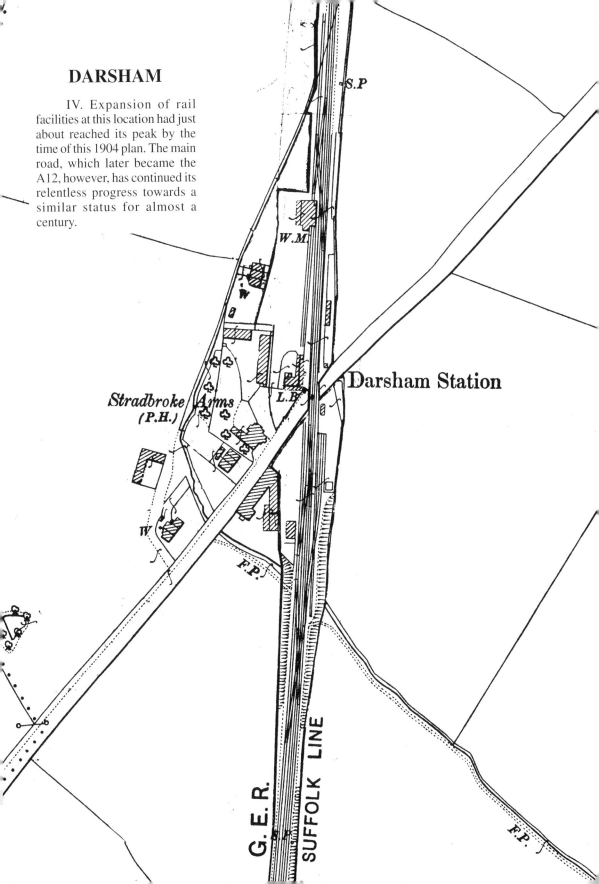

S.P

W.M

Darsham Station

L.B

Stradbroke Arms
(P.H.)

W

F.P.

F.P.

G. E. R.

SUFFOLK LINE

F.P.

4.   The goods yard appears to be thriving, as we look south from the signalbox in October 1911. Ten coal wagons, of varying profiles, stand in the siding serving Thurtell & Co's coal shed on the right, whilst a cattle truck and three horse boxes occupy the cattle dock to the left. The two bolster wagons in the centre are more unexpected in this rural location – maybe a local farmer has just taken delivery of some heavy piece of agricultural machinery. (HMRS, Hilton Collection)

5.   An up train causes little inconvenience to road traffic as it pulls away over the level crossing during the early years of the twentieth century. The imposing station building is larger than one would expect for a village of some 400 inhabitants. (R.K.Blencowe)

6.   A goods shed at the north end of the down platform supplemented the siding facilities to the south of the level crossing. In this 1953 picture, a class B12 4-6-0 is heading an empty stock train past the goods shed towards the Great Eastern signal by the level crossing. Goods facilities were withdrawn on 19th April 1965. (Stations UK)

7.   The village lies a mile or so to the east of the station, so most travellers on the A12 trunk road know it only by the level crossing. This fact was acknowledged and accepted by the villagers when it came to choosing a design for the village sign. (R.J.Adderson)

8.   Loco hauled trains on this section of the line were very rare indeed after the through London services ceased in May 1984. The photographer was therefore fortunate to be able to record green-liveried 37216 standing alongside the overgrown remains of the cattle dock with a permanent way train on 26th November 1992. Apart from the loss of one chimney stack, the exterior of the station building had changed little in almost a century. (D.C.Pearce)

9.   Again we see the 16.27 from Liverpool Street on 9th September 2000, as it crosses the A12 and slows for the station stop. The sign on the up platform shelter emphasises the precautions taken to protect the busy level crossing. (D.C.Pearce)

SOUTH OF HALESWORTH

10.   At first glance this is a somewhat unremarkable picture of the railway making its way across the countryside. However, closer inspection will reveal the abandoned 3 ft gauge tracks of the Southwold Railway, almost lost in the weeds as they run parallel to the main line on the east side of the embankment. For 50 years until 1929 this 9-mile long line connected the coastal town with the main line at Halesworth. The railway lay derelict throughout the 1930s, before being dismantled as part of the war effort in 1941. (R.Shephard)

11.   The photographer has now turned round, and we are looking north from much the same spot, with the road access to the goods yard on the right of the picture. Just out of the picture, the narrow gauge lines swing round towards their terminus on the east side of the goods yard. (R.Shephard)

12.   The bridge carrying the Southwold Railway over Holton Road survived until the early 1960s. It can be seen to the left of the picture as class D16/3 4-4-0 no.62546 *Claud Hamilton* slows for the station stop with a down express on 10th October 1956. (R.C.Riley)

Lodge

Patrick Stead Hospital

HALESWORTH

W

Allotment Gardens

4 ft. R.H.

Station Hotel

4 ft. R.H.

Station

98

Allotment Gardens

F.P.

Station

Elm

Malthouse

Def.

4 ft. R.H.

S.P

Allotment Gardens

Und.

4 ft. R.H.
Def.
4 ft. R.H.

Bapt. C.

Allotment Garden

W

P.H.

S.P.

Holton Terrace

Morty. (Ch. of

C.R.

School

L.B. B.P.

V. The comprehensive, but compact, nature of this location is shown to advantage in this 1904 plan. At this time, all the general goods generated by a small market town, including livestock, was dealt with, together with interchange traffic for the Southwold Railway. The latter had its station on the east side of the main line station, arriving from the coast via its own bridge over Holton Road at the southern end. Although there is little discernible difference at this scale, the Southwold was constructed to 3'-0" gauge; it closed in 1929. The refuge siding at the northern edge of the plan continued for nearly 300 yards. Other views of this station appear in Branch Line to Southwold.

G. E. R.
EAST SUFFOLK

13.   Early in the twentieth century an up train runs into the station and approaches the swinging platform section which had been installed when the platform was extended northwards across the road in 1887. We can date the picture by the raw earth on the cutting side, resulting from the construction of the up refuge siding in 1901. The Great Eastern enamel sign proclaims "Halesworth, Junction for Southwold". (R.K.Blencowe collection)

14.   On an October day in 1911 the goods yard is full of wagons, and the locomotive of the down freight has left part of its train on the main line while it shunts the yard. To the right, a Great Eastern ventilated van provides variety amongst the ubiquitous open wagons and box vans. (HMRS, Hilton Collection)

15.   Here we see the footbridge from which the previous photograph was taken. This picture dates from the 1930s, by which time the left hand span, providing access to the Southwold Railway station, was redundant. It was later dismantled, leaving the right hand span to link the platforms for another three decades. (R.Shephard)

16.   A few pedestrians hurry across the tracks as the railwayman closes the crossing to road traffic on a sunny day in the 1930s. The swinging platform sections seen here had been built by Boulton & Paul of Norwich in 1922 to replace the 1887 structure. (R.Shephard)

17.   An upper storey window in the milk depot provides a fine view of the goods yard and the countryside to the south in the 1950s, when freight traffic was still thriving. The goods yard closed on 19th April 1965, but the signal box was rescued when it became redundant in 1986 and was moved bodily to the grounds of a nearby school. (P. Punchard collection)

18.   A British Railways lorry stands in the station forecourt between trips to deliver and pick up consignments in the town and surrounding villages. This was one of a number of vehicles which ranged as far afield as Laxfield and Southwold during the late 1950s and early 1960s. The upper storey of the station building had been only partially rebuilt following air raid damage during World War 2. (P. Punchard collection)

19.   For many years the volume of goods traffic justified the provision of a shunting locomotive, which ran a total of 34 unproductive miles light engine to and from Lowestoft each day to perform its duties. It also had to run to and from Darsham in the early afternoon when required to shunt there. In 1952 the engine was booked to leave Lowestoft at 6.10 am, and it did not get back until 4.40 pm. Class E4 2-4-0 no.62797 was the locomotive performing this accountant's nightmare on 10th October 1956. (R.C.Riley)

20.   By the 1950s, the level crossing was causing delays to the ever-increasing road traffic, and eventually the road was diverted over a new bridge to the north of the platforms. This was the scene from the station footbridge just before the crossing was abolished in 1959. Milk traffic is still booming, whilst the sign suspended from the canopy on the left states "Cycling on these premises prohibited" (R.J.Adderson)

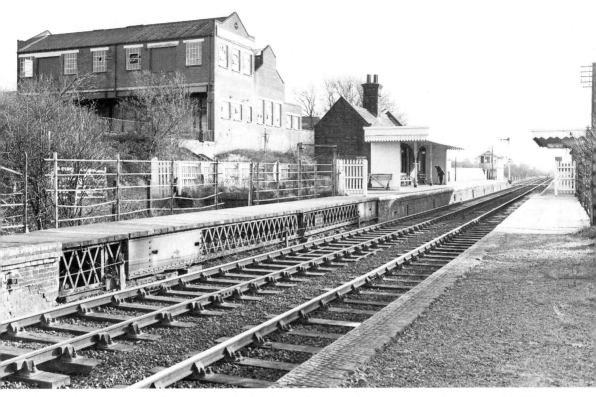

21.   Once the new road had opened, the level crossing was left permanently closed to road traffic, forming part of an unbroken platform. The winter sun highlights the ironwork on 15th January 1975. By the signal box, the footbridge has vanished, but somebody still cares enough to sweep the platform. (British Rail)

22.   The relationship with Southwold was perpetuated long after the narrow gauge line was swept away. Until 1965 a timetable footnote emphasised that Halesworth was the "Station for Southwold", and as late as 26th July 1980, the station nameboard still proclaimed this fact. (R.J.Adderson)

23.   The decaying platform and rusting mechanism of the old level crossing were removed for cosmetic restoration in 1999, as part of a facelift programme which also saw the station building refurbished in order to house the town museum. For a few weeks that summer the wheels on which the swinging section revolved were revealed to passers-by. (R.J.Adderson)

24.   The elevated vantage-point of the road bridge emphasises just how much the railway has contracted, with trees encroaching on the platforms to the north of the level crossing. In the distance, housing development occupies the site of the former dairy, goods yard and narrow gauge lines, leaving just the double track through the platforms. A class 150 pauses on its way to Ipswich in July 2000. (G.L.Kenworthy)

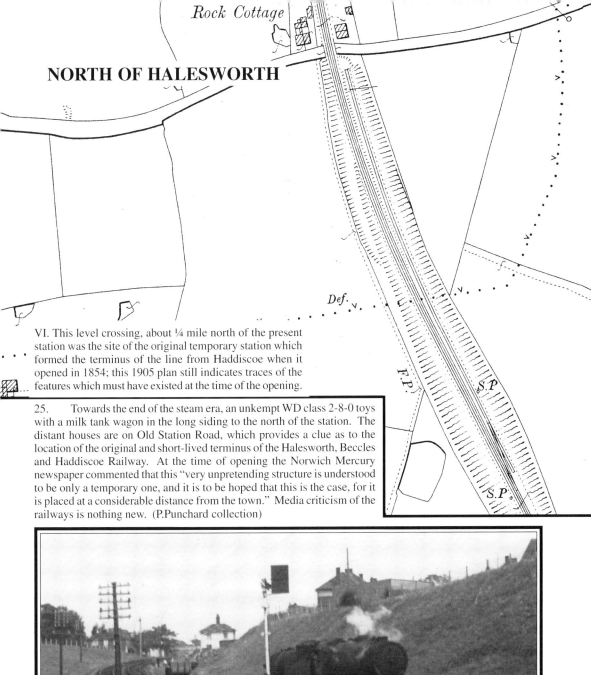

NORTH OF HALESWORTH

Rock Cottage

Def.

F.P.

S.P.

S.P.

VI. This level crossing, about ¼ mile north of the present station was the site of the original temporary station which formed the terminus of the line from Haddiscoe when it opened in 1854; this 1905 plan still indicates traces of the features which must have existed at the time of the opening.

25. Towards the end of the steam era, an unkempt WD class 2-8-0 toys with a milk tank wagon in the long siding to the north of the station. The distant houses are on Old Station Road, which provides a clue as to the location of the original and short-lived terminus of the Halesworth, Beccles and Haddiscoe Railway. At the time of opening the Norwich Mercury newspaper commented that this "very unpretending structure is understood to be only a temporary one, and it is to be hoped that this is the case, for it is placed at a considerable distance from the town." Media criticism of the railways is nothing new. (P.Punchard collection)

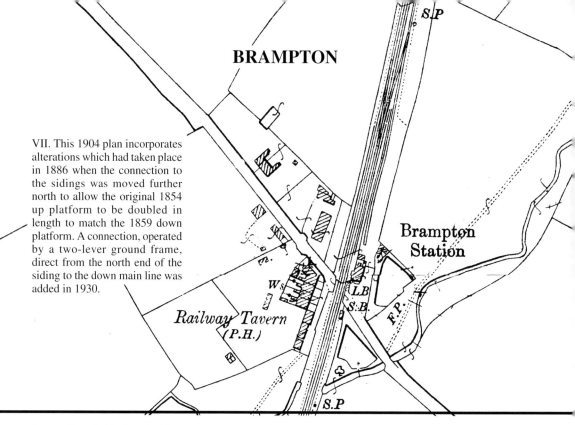

BRAMPTON

VII. This 1904 plan incorporates alterations which had taken place in 1886 when the connection to the sidings was moved further north to allow the original 1854 up platform to be doubled in length to match the 1859 down platform. A connection, operated by a two-lever ground frame, direct from the north end of the siding to the down main line was added in 1930.

Brampton Station

Railway Tavern (P.H.)

26.   Even in black and white, we can appreciate the colourful flowerbeds on the down platform, as class J39 0-6-0 no.2771 propels wagons into the yard on a Summer day between the wars. The GER "Brampton" running-in board has been supplemented by another board confirming the Suffolk location - it is doubtful whether many passengers would have confused this location with Brampton in Cumberland, but the LNER was obviously taking no chances! (P.Punchard collection)

27.   Class B1 4-6-0 no. 61399 runs north through the station with a Royal Train on the morning of 2nd May 1956. It is carrying the Duke of Edinburgh to Lowestoft, where he was due to open the South Pier Pavilion and to tour the shipyards. (NRS Archive)

28.   Goods facilities were limited, but were no doubt adequate for the traffic that the village generated. Looking north on 31st August 1963 we see the single siding serving the cattle pen, and the loading gauge over the siding behind the up platform. The view was destined to last for less than a year as the goods yard was closed on 13th July 1964. (G.L.Kenworthy collection)

29.   In October 1886 a Board of Trade Inspecting Officer commented "I was sorry to observe that there is no shelter on the down platform". This omission was not rectified until 1959/60, when a waiting shelter was moved here from Great Ormesby. The long-awaited facility had only just been installed when this picture was taken. (NRS Archive)

30.   The station building and level crossing are seen to good effect as a class 37 diesel pauses with an up train in the early 1960s. Within a few years the station building would be demolished, leaving the up platform devoid of any shelter. (P.Punchard collection)

31.   A class 150 arrives at the former up platform with a train from Ipswich in July 2000. We can see that the down platform has been demolished to make way for car parking following the 1980s resignalling. Remarkably the nomadic waiting shelter again outlasted the platform on which it stood, and has been preserved at Mangapps Farm in Essex. (G.L.Kenworthy)

BECCLES BANK

In 1885 a signal box and crossover were provided at this location so that heavy trains could be banked at the rear on the 1 in 87 southbound climb out of Beccles. Until that date the pilot engine was attached to the front of the train and had to run through to Saxmundham before returning to Beccles for its next duty. The location of the signal box is shown on the gradient diagram; it survived until 1958, when it was destroyed by fire.

32. "Sandringham" class 4-6-0 no.61629 *Naworth Castle* passes the neat little signal box as it tackles the last few yards of the long climb out of Beccles with the 6.18 pm from Yarmouth on 3rd May 1957. By this time the signal box was rarely used and the crossover had been removed. The gradient post indicates the summit, which is followed by a downhill stretch of 1 in 90. (The late E.Alger/Colourail)

33.   A class 150 heads for Ipswich at nearby Weston level crossing. The site of Beccles Bank signalbox is in the distance, at the top of the gradient. The switchback nature of the line hereabouts is clearly illustrated in this view, dating from the summer of 2000. (G.L.Kenworthy)

Works
(ting)

BECCLES

Auction

LANCASTER PLACE

S.Ps

...ATION ROAD

Chap.

Hospital

FAIRCLOSE ROAD

Ingate Iron Works

P.H.

LB

P.H.

S.P

Malthouse

GOSFORD ROAD

B.M.13·6

13

S.P

Station
Junction for Lowestoft and Bungay

EAST SUFFOLK LINE

G. E. R.

BEC

F.B.

S.B

F.B

Cr.

S.P

F.B

dge

te

use

S.P

...STREET

P.H.

P.H.

A T E   R O A D

G.P.

11

ROAD

VIII. This plan dating from 1905 demonstrates that Beccles was the largest intermediate community served by the East Suffolk Railway. The complex layout is notable; it was required to serve the many traders of this important agricultural centre and to enable the splitting and joining of main line trains to and from the coastal resorts of Lowestoft and Yarmouth. The Waveney Valley line swings away to the west from the northern end of the down platform, while the branch to Lowestoft runs parallel to the main line for about ¼ mile before turning east towards the coast.

5

Sewage Pits

nt to which
Tides flow

B E C

F.B.

s Works

F.B.

F.B.

Sluices

F.B.

Sewage Works
(Beccles Corporation)

S.P.

S.P.

Common Lane Cross

S.B.

Engine Shed

S.P.

S.P.

RK

ROAD

Tank

S.Ps

S.P.

S.B.

P.H.

34.   The large goods shed is a prominent feature of this 1911 view northwards from the signalbox towards the busy goods yard and the station. (HMRS, Hilton Collection)

35.   We have now moved 100 yards or so closer to the station on the same day, with the signal indicating that a down train cannot be very far away. Beyond the gate on the extreme left of the picture, at least three Midland Railway wagons are standing on the siding which ran unprotected across the station forecourt. (HMRS, Hilton Collection)

36.   Here we have the opportunity to share a relaxed moment with some of the station staff. The postcard bears a 1913 postmark, but even then showed a historic scene, as the station building had been extended during the previous year, with the loss of the porch and its arched entrance. The walled passageway to the left carries a public footpath across the railway, and is quaintly described as a "perambulator bridge" on a contemporary GER plan. (G.L.Kenworthy collection)

37.   Class D15 4-4-0 no.8783 heads away from the station, past South signal box, with an up express in early LNER days. The vans and cattle wagon in front of the coaches remind us that passenger traffic was not the only priority at the time (R.J.Adderson collection)

38.   The lines serving the engine shed at the north end of the complex were still used into the diesel era, although no engines had been allocated here since the mid 1940s. A class J15 0-6-0 stands outside the shed as a new Brush Type 2 diesel passes with an up passenger train, whose first two vehicles are an LNER articulated set. The shed had been built in 1888 to replace an earlier structure adjacent to the South signal box. (NRS Archive)

39.   Two class J15 0-6-0s stand outside the distant engine shed as class N7 0-6-2T no. 69690 propels a two-coach push pull set out of the station, again during the late 1950s. Stopping trains such as this served the intermediate stations on the Yarmouth line in between the express workings. (NRS Archive)

40.   A distinctive feature of the station was the 6-ft wide timber "swing bridge" which connected the up platform with the south end of the island platform. It had been installed in 1933 to facilitate the movement of milk churns and barrows, and when not in use it was housed in a recess in the island platform, becoming part of the platform surface. On this occasion it had been swung across the tracks to enable an oil drum to be moved from the island platform. The contraption was controlled from a ground frame, which was in turn released from the South signal box. (J.Watling)

41.   The barrow bridge was pivoted at the north end, whilst the outer end was guided by a carrying wheel running on a curved rail attached to the sleepers. This arrangement provides a foreground to no D5515, as it stands at the platform with an up express in the late 1950s. (NRS Archive)

42. Class L1 2-6-4T no. 67709 provides some warmth for its crew on a wintry 25th January 1958. The water tower to the right of the picture marks the approximate site of the original engine shed, and we can see the ground frame controlling the barrow bridge at the end of the platform. (B.W.L.Brooksbank/Initial Photographics)

43. By contrast it is a warm 1950s Summer afternoon as a class J15 0-6-0 stands at the GER bracket signal on the goods lines to the east of the station. The nearer bridge carries the public footpath: the steps of the adjacent station footbridge, which had by now lost the canopy seen in picture number 35, are just beyond it. (NRS Archive)

44.   From certain angles, the footbridges could obscure a driver's view of the up starter signal, so two arms were provided at different levels – a feature that survived until the radio signalling was introduced. In 1959, the signals were still of GER design, and were supplemented by a calling-on arm for use when the Yarmouth and Lowestoft portions of up trains were combined, a regular part of operations here. (NRS Archive)

45.   Having arrived in platform 3 with the 11.35 am train from Yarmouth on 30th October 1959, "Britannia" class 4-6-2 no.70008 *Black Prince* has been uncoupled and has reversed into platform 4 to pick up the Lowestoft portion, which had arrived two minutes earlier. The next move will be to add these coaches to the front of the train, before setting out for London. At this time the timetable allowed only 11 minutes between the arrival of the Lowestoft coaches and the departure of the combined train. (G.L.Kenworthy collection)

46. Division of down trains was a far simpler process. The through coaches for Lowestoft were uncoupled from the rear of the train during the station stop, and once the Yarmouth train had left, another engine would back on to the remaining two or three coaches for the last 8½ miles of their journey to the Suffolk coast. On this occasion in the late 1950s, passengers for Lowestoft will arrive at their destination behind class J15 0-6-0 no. 65460. We can only conjecture what the railwayman is saying to the nun! (NRS Archive)

47. The starter signal confirms that "Britannia" class 4-6-2 no. 70038 *Robin Hood* will be taking the Yarmouth line, as it waits to leave on the last leg of its journey with the 12.38 pm from Liverpool Street on 27th October 1959. The other arms on the gantry control departures for the Waveney Valley line and Lowestoft; the former route can be seen curving to the west behind Beccles North signalbox,. (G.L.Kenworthy collection)

48.   A few passengers are waiting for the 07.17 from Lowestoft to Liverpool Street, as it arrives behind no.37049 on 12ᵗʰ May 1984. This train, together with the return working in the evening, was a reminder of more prosperous times. However, this was the last day of the through London service, and the locomotive is carrying a headboard to mark the occasion. (R.J.Adderson)

49.   Since the resignalling, there has been just a single track through the station, surrounded by decaying relics of the past. A solitary passenger waits for an up train as it runs in past the abandoned island platform in the early 1990s. The train is formed of a three car class 101 DMU, one of several fitted with radio signalling equipment and which monopolised services over the East Suffolk line at the time. (R.J.Adderson)

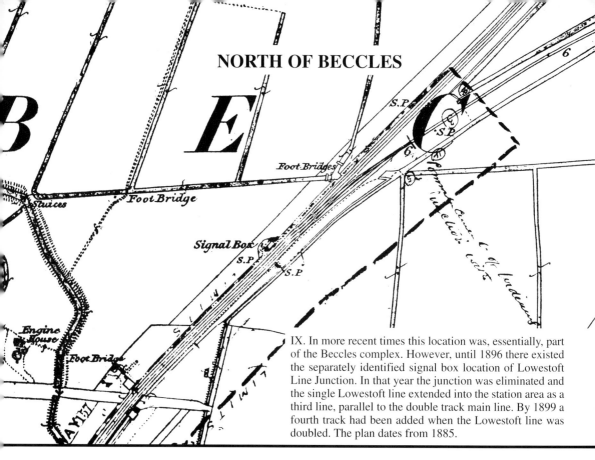

IX. In more recent times this location was, essentially, part of the Beccles complex. However, until 1896 there existed the separately identified signal box location of Lowestoft Line Junction. In that year the junction was eliminated and the single Lowestoft line extended into the station area as a third line, parallel to the double track main line. By 1899 a fourth track had been added when the Lowestoft line was doubled. The plan dates from 1885.

50.   The double tracks to Yarmouth and Lowestoft ran parallel for some distance to the north of the station. Looking out from a class B1 hauled train heading for Yarmouth on 28th February 1959, it would appear that we are on an important stretch of quadruple tracked main line! (A.E.Bennett)

BECCLES SWING BRIDGE

51.   The 1854 – built bridge has been swung to enable a pleasure wherry to make its stately way up the Waveney. This picture was sold locally as a postcard, probably around 1900. In earlier years a signal box on each side of the river had controlled interlaced tracks across the bridge, but this somewhat unusual feature was replaced in 1892 by a more conventional single-track arrangement. (R.J.Adderson collection)

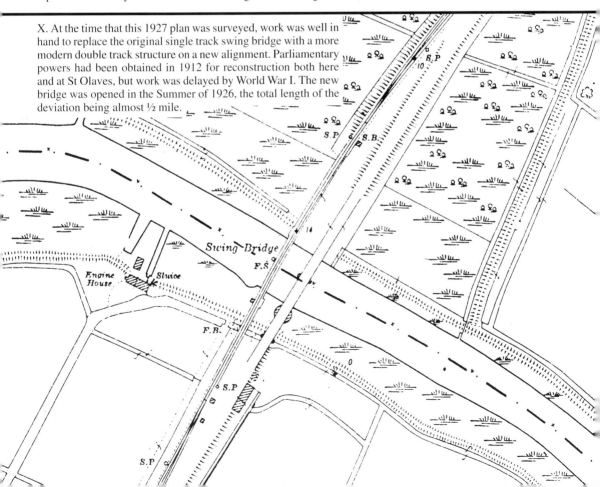

X. At the time that this 1927 plan was surveyed, work was well in hand to replace the original single track swing bridge with a more modern double track structure on a new alignment. Parliamentary powers had been obtained in 1912 for reconstruction both here and at St Olaves, but work was delayed by World War I. The new bridge was opened in the Summer of 1926, the total length of the deviation being almost ½ mile.

52.   The piers of the new bridge were taking shape when the official photographer visited the site on 17th September 1925. Men and machinery are hard at work, and a primitive narrow gauge line lurches unsteadily across the muddy site. The north signal cabin can be made out between the two bridges, on the far bank of the river. (British Railways)

53.   Five months have gone by, and the fixed spans of the replacement structure have been installed, dwarfing their predecessor to the west. The name of the contracting engineers, The Horseley Bridge & Engineering Co Ltd, is painted on the steelwork. (National Railway Museum)

SOUTHERN AREA, GE SECTION BRIDGE No 476
BETWEEN BECCLES AND ALDEBY AT 110m 55c.
GENERAL VIEW FROM BECCLES END
17.9.25.   No 1659.

54.   When the official photographer returned on 9th June 1926, he found the swinging span in place and the signal box taking shape, and set up his equipment on the very edge of the old bridge to record developments on the south bank of the river. Six weeks later the Inspector expressed his satisfaction with the completed scheme, and reported that the new 230-ton span took about two minutes to swing. By the time it was complete, the whole project had cost the LNER £89424. (British Railways)

SOUTHERN AREA SECTION BECCLES & HADDISCOE
BRIDGE No. 478 AT HOM 55¼ GENERAL VIEW
FROM BECCLES END No. 1725A

55.   A class J17 0-6-0 trundles across the bridge with a down goods train in the late 1950s. Unless he had a boat the photographer would have faced a long trek across marshland tracks to reach this spot, for there was no road access. (NRS Archive)

56.   The original bridge had lasted for 72 years, but the new structures were destined to survive for less than half that time. With the bridge to the left, the signal box, power house and battery house cluster above the surrounding marshes on 27th October 1959, just five days before they were used for the last time. (G.L.Kenworthy collection)

57.   By rail it was just under four miles between the swing bridges at Beccles and St Olaves, but the river described a semi-circle to the east, and flowed over 10 miles between the two bridges. There were three level crossings in quick succession south of Aldeby, taking country lanes across the railway to the villages of Burgh St Peter and Wheatacre, isolated in the great loop of the Waveney. At the most southerly of the crossings, the gatekeeper and cyclist are probably discussing the impending closure. (G.L.Kenworthy collection)

58.   Not far to the north, a similar gatehouse controlled the middle crossing, which lay at the south end of a sharp curve. This picture, like the previous one, dates from 29th October 1959, only three days before this section of line was closed completely. Although much extended, both these buildings survived into the 21st century as private dwellings. (G.L.Kenworthy collection)

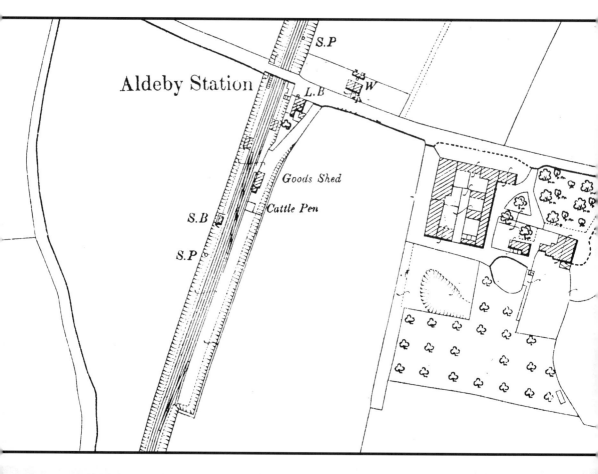

Aldeby Station

S.P

L.B

W

Goods Shed

Cattle Pen

S.B

S.P

XI. This 1905 plan shows the connection that had been laid in 1900 (opposite the signal box) to connect the siding with the down main line; prior to that date it had only been accessible from the up line. The layout remained unaltered at the time of closure to passengers.

59.   Looking north from the down platform on a Summer's day around 1930, we see the epitome of the village railway station. The impeccably maintained platforms, neat waiting shelters and the old coach body combine with the barrows to produce a traditional atmosphere – there is even a milk churn below the lamp on the extreme right. (Stations UK)

60.   A similar viewpoint dating from 25th June 1959 reveals several changes. The platform buildings have been replaced by more functional structures, whilst the steps down from the road bridge have been replaced by a sloping access path. However, the tree in the centre of the picture continues to shield the main station building from view. (G.L.Kenworthy collection)

61. "Britannia" class 4-6-2 no.70002 *Geoffrey Chaucer* speeds through the station with an up express in the Summer of 1959. The first vehicle is an ex-GER buffet car, still in main line service some 36 years after the GER ceased to exist. We now have the opportunity to see the station building, at road level to the east of the bridge. (Stations UK)

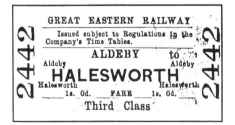

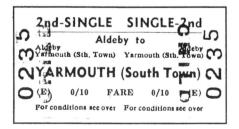

62.   A large sign on the frontage of the building informed road users that they were passing the station – a feature that we shall see again before reaching the end of our journey. The platform is beginning to show signs of neglect on 25th June 1959. (G.L.Kenworthy collection)

G. E. R.

From

TO

ALDEBY

63.   "Britannia" class 4-6-2 no.70030 *William Wordsworth* passes the signal box and empty goods yard with a down express in April 1959. Goods traffic may have been light in the Spring, but the volume of sugar beet handled in Autumn and Winter was sufficient to keep the goods yard open until the end of 1964. (B.Reading)

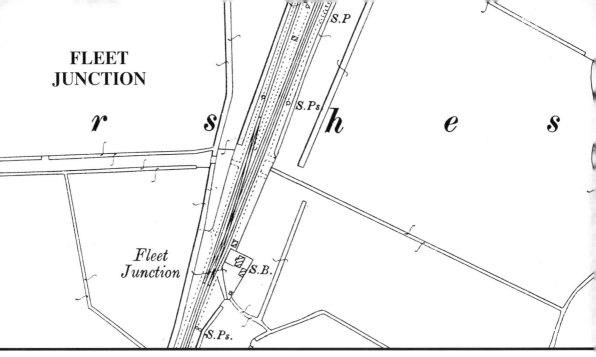

FLEET JUNCTION

r   *s*   *h*   *e*   *s*

S.P

S.Ps

Fleet Junction

S.B.

S.Ps.

XII. It was from this point that, in 1859, the East Suffolk line was opened northwards from the original route of the Halesworth, Beccles and Haddiscoe Railway, opened five years earlier.

64.   The fireman looks out from the cab of class B1 4-6-0 no.61056 as it approaches the lonely junction signal box with the 3.38 pm train from Ipswich on 18th July 1959. Ahead of him is the climb to Haddiscoe High Level station and the higher ground to the north of the river. (G.L.Kenworthy collection)

65.   The former Halesworth, Beccles and Haddiscoe main line, now just a freight spur, heads across the marshes towards Haddiscoe Low Level station, which can be seen to the left of the signals. This picture was taken from a down train on 5ᵗʰ September 1959. (G.L.Kenworthy collection)

66.   Following the closure of the main line, an occasional goods train to Aldeby continued to use the connecting line, which is on the right of this picture. This scene can be dated around 1960, when the Aldeby freights ran on the former up line and the down main line was used for storing wagons. The double track towards Yarmouth is out of use, although the signal box and crossover are still in place. (NRS Archive)

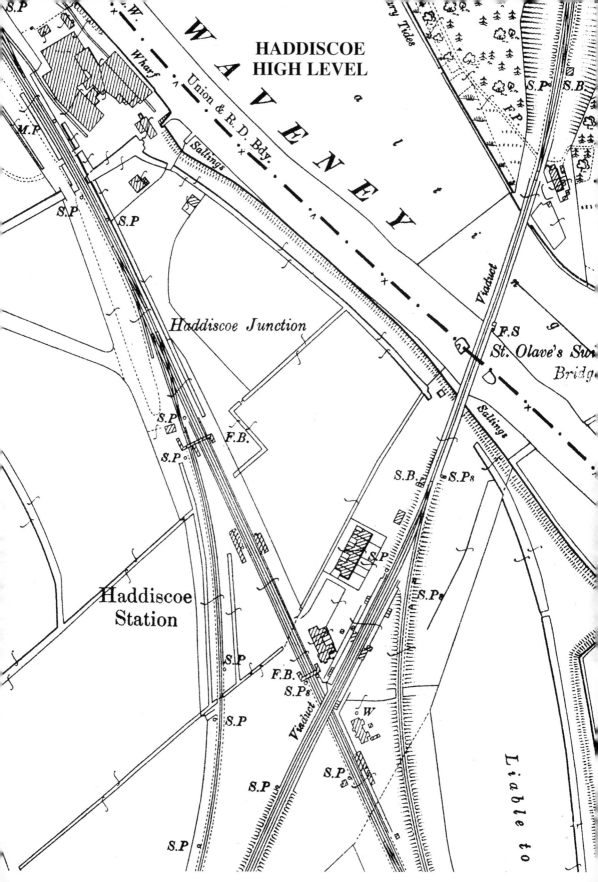

HADDISCOE
HIGH LEVEL

W A V E N E Y

Wharf

Union & R.D. Bdy.

Saltings

M.P.

S.P.

S.P.

Haddiscoe Junction

F.S

St. Olave's Sw
Bridg

Viaduct

Saltings

S.P.

S.P.

F.B.

S.B.

S.Ps

S.P

S.Ps

Haddiscoe
Station

S.P

S.P

S.P.

F.B.

S.Ps

W

Viaduct

S.P

S.P

S.Ps

S.P

S.P

S.B.

FP

S.P

Liable to

XIII. From the 1859 opening, this station was provided purely to provide an interchange with services on the low level line between Norwich and Lowestoft. It was known variously as St Olaves Junction and Herringfleet Junction; there was even a proposal, in 1879, to call it St Olaves Bridge. On 9th May 1904, the original Haddiscoe station, located on the low level line just beyond the western edge of this plan, was closed in connection with improvements on that route. The new interchange assumed the name of Haddiscoe from that date and this 1905 plan shows the subsequent station arrangements.

To the north of the station, the location of the first swing bridge is also shown; it was, in common with other similar 19th century structures, constructed for a single track only. The staff cottages to the north-east of the bridge were demolished to make way for the new track alignment which was necessary when the bridge was reconstructed in the 1920s. The new bridge opened in 1927, almost a year after the similar structure at Beccles.

67.	Whilst the other stations on the line fitted snugly into their communities, this was simply an exchange station, perched high above the marshes a mile or more from the village it purported to serve, and the facilities provided reflected this function. We are looking north along the wooden platforms in the early 1920s, towards the original swing bridge. Beyond the platforms, a junction signal controls the line to Marsh Junction, and the signals on this north to east curve can be seen behind the fencing on the right of the picture. (Stations UK)

68.   The station was rebuilt in conjunction with the new swing bridge, but the facilities remained basic. Intending passengers had to make their way along the Low Level platform and up a ramp to reach the High Level, where a small waiting shelter on each platform was considered sufficient for their needs. Again, we are looking north, this time on 25th June 1959. A comparison with the previous picture suggests that the shelter on the left, above the railway cottages, had survived all the changes. (G.L.Kenworthy collection)

69.   The exposed situation of the station is apparent as class B1 4-6-0 no. 61329 reaches the top of the short but sharp climb from Fleet Junction with the 9.38 am from Liverpool Street on the same day. To the right of the picture we see the footbridge at the Low Level station. (J.E.Dean)

70.   An hour or so earlier, "Britannia" class 4-6-2 no. 70012 *John of Gaunt* approaches the north end of the High Level platform with the 11.35 am from Yarmouth to Liverpool Street. With only five coaches, it will have no difficulty in picking up speed after the 30 m.p.h. slack over the swing bridge, but its power will be fully utilised over the gradients south of Beccles after the Lowestoft portion has been added. The modern locomotive contrasts with the gas lamp and tall Great Eastern signal. (G.L.Kenworthy collection)

ST.OLAVES SWING BRIDGE

71.   Seemingly marooned on the swinging span of the original bridge, a railway employee watches as a yacht makes its way up river, during the early years of the twentieth century. At this time holidaymakers were just beginning to discover the charms of the waterways of Norfolk and North Suffolk. (M.Storey-Smith collection)

72.   On the 27th July 1923 the Chief Civil Engineer wrote, "The condition of the St Olaves Bridge has become such that its reconstruction must be taken in hand immediately". Looking at this photograph of the 64-year-old structure from the south-east, taken the previous day, it is easy to understand his concern! A red flag warns shipping that the bridge is open to rail traffic. (National Railway Museum)

73.   In addition to the structural limitations of the bridge, the single track across it was a major operating inconvenience. Until 1909 the tracks had been interlaced across the bridge, and for the next 17 years the signal boxes at each end of the bridge controlled trains over a short single-track section. Here we see St Olaves Swing Bridge Junction signal box, on the south bank of the river, as it was on 26th July 1923. The photographer is standing on the line to Marsh Junction, and the main line on the left becomes single track beside the signal box. (National Railway Museum)

74.   We have now crossed to the north bank of the river, where the double track resumed at St Olaves Swing Bridge North signal box. On 2nd September 1924 the remodelling work is well under way, and the widened cutting is a raw scar on the face of the landscape. The main lines were later realigned through the site of the signal box, while the engineers wagons are standing on an extended siding running from St Olaves goods yard. (British Railways)

75. No words can do justice to this superb view of the area taken from the north bank of the river during the rebuilding work. We can only urge the reader to study the picture in conjunction with the map, and to savour the details it illustrates! (National Railway Museum)

76.   Seen from the signalbox, class D15 4-4-0 no.8799 heads north over the river. This photograph was taken during a visit by members of the Norwich Engineering Society shortly after the new bridge had been completed. At this time the signalbox boasted no fewer than 56 levers, of which 35 were spare, because it was originally intended to control the whole Haddiscoe complex, both High and Low Level, from here. (A.S.Harrison, courtesy B. Harrison)

77.   The tidy appearance of the new bridge, with its steel approach spans, was probably best appreciated from the river on a warm sunny day. It was quite a contrast with the timber trestles and fragile looking structure of its predecessor. (G.L.Kenworthy collection)

78.   A Derby Lightweight DMU on a Beccles to Yarmouth service comes off the north end of the bridge shortly before the line closed. The final timetable shows that diesel units operated most stopping trains on weekdays, but by then there were few passengers to enjoy the "drivers-eye" view of the swing bridges that they offered. (NRS Archive)

79.   The last working over the bridge took place on 28th June 1961, when D2553 rumbled across with a demolition train, and it was dismantled soon afterwards. However, the brick built piers survived, like giant stepping-stones across the river and the surrounding marshland. A holiday cruiser has just passed the circular pivot pier, as we look northwards on 2nd June 1974. Long after the railway had vanished, British Railways remained responsible for maintaining the navigation light seen on the pier in the middle of the river. (R.J.Adderson)

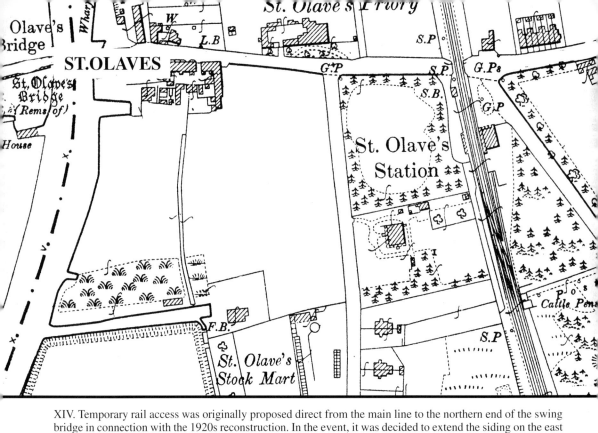

XIV. Temporary rail access was originally proposed direct from the main line to the northern end of the swing bridge in connection with the 1920s reconstruction. In the event, it was decided to extend the siding on the east side of the line in this 1905 plan southwards to the swing bridge to avoid the complications of a running line connection.

80.   Here we see the station looking southwards from the level crossing around 1900. The signalman leans proudly from his box, whilst three members of the station staff pose for the camera on the up platform. (Lens of Sutton)

81.   We are now looking northwards from the elevated viewpoint of the up advance starter signal towards the station in October 1911. The headshunt by the hut beyond the footpath crossing was later extended into the lengthy siding which we saw in picture 74. Further north, the down platform and goods yard entrance are visible, but the up platform and building are hidden by the trees. (HMRS, Hilton collection)

82.   It is late March 1955, and the Spring sunshine warms the signal box and level crossing gates. The sign by the road survived the closure, and at the time of writing it can still be seen on the wall of a nearby garage. (Eastern Counties Newspapers)

83.   Class C12 4-4-2T no.67366 rolls over the level crossing into the station with a stopping train from Yarmouth to Beccles in 1956. The neighbouring village of Fritton merits a mention on the running-in board, as it had since Great Eastern days. (P.Hay)

84.   Two wagons of sugar beet await collection from the siding on 24th October 1959. They are bound for Cantley factory, some seven miles away as the crow flies, but would have a circuitous journey via Yarmouth South Town before reaching their destination. The yard remained available to sugar beet traffic until the end of the 1959/60 campaign. (J.E.Dean)

85.   Although it had been laid specifically for use in connection with the 1920s rebuilding work, the long siding to the south of the station remained in place to the end, and was being used to stable some 40 container wagons on 24th October 1959. The swing bridge is just out of sight, round the curve in the distance. The tall bracket signal provides a link with the past, for the left-hand post once carried a signal controlling the line to Marsh Junction. (G.L.Kenworthy collection)

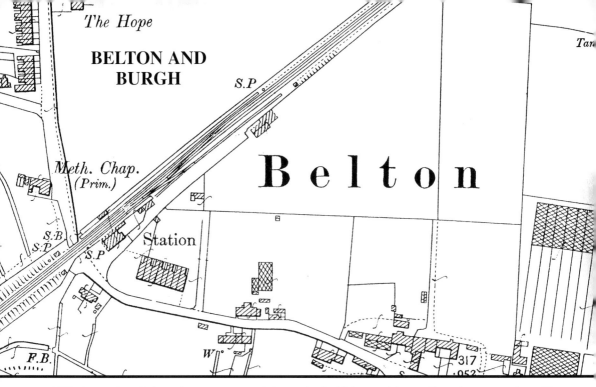

XV. Opened as Belton, improvement of the early facilities at this small station were slow. The original, and only, siding provided, remained as shown in this 1906 plan until it was finally extended northwards by 400 feet in 1929; it was provided with a new connection to the down main line at the same time.

86.   A view southward from the tall down starter signal reveals the station and goods yard as they were in October 1911. Beyond the open wagons, a GNR 6-wheel van stands at the far end of the siding. This was almost certainly being loaded with boxes of chrysanthemums, grown in nearby glasshouses, some of which appear as diamond cross-hatching on the lower right of the map. (HMRS, Hilton Collection)

87.   The station changed only in detail over the years. Looking north from the level crossing in the early 1920s, we can see enamel advertising signs, the gradient post on the platform, and the massive crossing gate post – none of these items appear in later pictures. (Stations UK)

88.   A large enamel sign on the south wall of the station building reminds us that the station was renamed in July 1923, shortly after the GER became part of the LNER. This photograph was taken in the late 1940s, and the white paint at the base of the protruding brickwork was a wartime measure to help visibility during the blackout. A comparison with the previous picture reveals that the rather tired looking brick platform facing had been replaced with smarter concrete components during the inter-war years. (G.L.Kenworthy collection)

89.   After nationalisation, the new owners went to the trouble of not only removing the LNER logo, but also moving the nameboard higher up the wall. Seen from the signalbox, no. D5539 runs light towards Beccles on 25th July 1959. (G.L.Kenworthy collection)

90.   With just over a week to go before closure, a "Britannia" class 4-6-2 speeds past the goods siding with the 11.35 am from Yarmouth to Liverpool Street on 23rd October 1959. The length of the down platform, with its distinctive pampas grass plants, is noteworthy – it had been extended northwards in 1898 and was used on occasions as a ticket platform for Yarmouth South Town. (J.E.Dean)

91.   There was no space to extend the short up platform, squeezed in between the siding and the level crossing. Its cramped location is emphasised in this picture, looking southwards from a passing train on 5th September 1959. The building nearest the camera was provided for a local trader in 1894, whilst the rectangular light coloured structure is an extension to the station house, approved at a cost of £115 in 1898 to help accommodate the stationmaster's large family. (J.E.Dean)

92.   The signal box, dating back to 1886, stood on the west side of the line to the south of the level crossing. It had replaced a previous building on the opposite side of the tracks, which survived as a lamp room until it was burnt down during World War 2. This picture too was taken shortly before the line closed. (J.E.Dean)

93.   On a dark winters evening, the signalman warms himself by the spotless "Guidwife" stove. The immaculate condition of the box owed much to Billy Squires, who had started on the railway as a lad porter at Belton around 1914 and was signalman there from 1945 until closure. It is difficult to imagine what his thoughts were as he worked the very last shift before the line closed. (D.W.Dean)

94.   As the down home signal was close to the south wall of the signalbox it was very difficult for the signalman to confirm the position of the signal arm. A small repeater arm was therefore provided on the signal post, level with the box windows. The repeater signal confirms that the road is clear for "Britannia" class 4-6-2 no.70038 *Robin Hood*, as it heads the 9.38 am from Liverpool Street up the 1 in 165 gradient towards the station on 23rd October 1959. (J.E.Dean)

95.   Work on lifting the track between St Olaves and Yarmouth started soon after the end of the 1959/60 sugar beet campaign. Just north of the station, a class J17 0-6-0 makes its way towards Yarmouth with a load of recovered track on 22nd June 1960. The village of Burgh Castle, with its Roman fort, lies a mile or so to the north west. (G.L.Kenworthy collection)

96.   The approach to South Town across the fields was the least dramatic of all the rail routes into Yarmouth, having nothing to compare with the glimpses of the North Sea enjoyed by passengers on the M&GN route, nor the sight of Breydon water next to Vauxhall station. About two miles north of Belton, the line emerged from a shallow cutting to provide passengers with their first glimpse of the distant town. Class F5 2-4-2T no.67199 heads south at this point with a stopping train from Yarmouth to Beccles on 2nd June 1951. (B.Reading)

97.   We are now approaching the end of our journey, and the embankment of the M&GN line from Yarmouth Beach station can be seen in the distance. The line had been disused since 1953, and was being used to store container wagons on 28th February 1959. (A.E.Bennett)

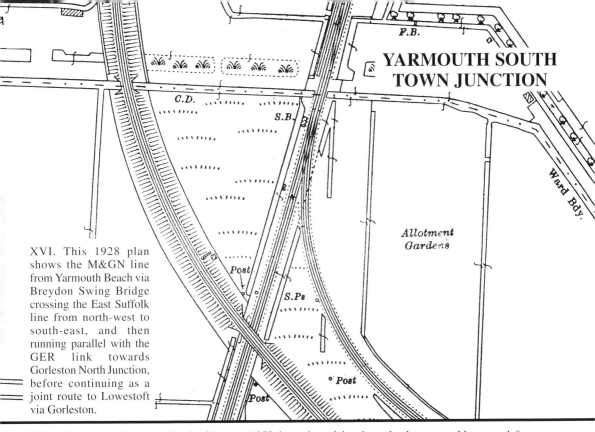

F.B.

C.D.

S.B.

Allotment Gardens

Ward Bdy.

Post

S.Ps

° Post

Post

Post

XVI. This 1928 plan shows the M&GN line from Yarmouth Beach via Breydon Swing Bridge crossing the East Suffolk line from north-west to south-east, and then running parallel with the GER link towards Gorleston North Junction, before continuing as a joint route to Lowestoft via Gorleston.

98.	During the disastrous floods of January 1953, it was hoped that the embankment would act as a defence against the onrushing water, and the bridge over the Beccles line had been blocked with sandbags in a vain effort to protect the nearby town. There is still plenty of water around as class B17 4-6-0 no. 61665 Leicester City heads south on 19th February 1953, the day that train services were resumed. (Eastern Counties Newspapers)

99.   A Derby Lightweight DMU has passed under the M&GN bridge and approaches the junction with the Lowestoft line in the late 1950s. Originally the junction was controlled by nearby Yarmouth South Town Junction signal box, but this was abolished around 1932. From then on, the junction points were motor-operated from the station box, about ¼ mile away. (NRS Archive)

100.   On the last day of the Lowestoft service, a class 105 DMU curves round towards the site of Gorleston North Junction. We are looking north along the trackbed of the Beccles line, with the one remaining wall of the former M&GN bridge on the left. These lingering reminders of the three routes at this point would soon disappear completely beneath new roads and industrial development. (R.J.Adderson)

**YARMOUTH
SOUTH TOWN**
Factory

REAT
MOUTH

Coal Yard

STATION ROAD

CATTLE MARKET

Timber Yard

EAST SUFFOLK LINE

L.N.E.R.

Allotment Gardens

Engine Shed

Allotment Gardens

XVII. Originally opened as a two platform terminus with modest goods facilities, this 1928 plan shows how expansion had taken place in keeping with the station's status as the town's main line station for London; additional facilities had also been necessary when the Norfolk and Suffolk Joint Committee's Line from Lowestoft via Gorleston opened in 1903.

101. A class Y14 0-6-0 stands on the turntable road on 26th September 1911, with two other locomotives in evidence in the shed yard. Again the photographer has taken advantage of a signal post to obtain a panoramic view. (HMRS, Hilton Collection)

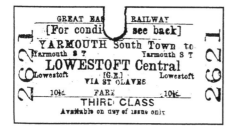

GREAT EASTERN RAILWAY
[For conditions see back]
YARMOUTH South Town to
Yarmouth S T   Yarmouth S T
LOWESTOFT Central
Lowestoft   [G.E.]   Lowestoft
VIA ST OLAVES
10½d   FARE   10½d
THIRD CLASS
Available on day of issue only
2621   2621

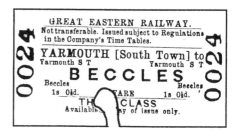

GREAT EASTERN RAILWAY.
Not transferable. Issued subject to Regulations
in the Company's Time Tables.
YARMOUTH [South Town] to
Yarmouth S T   Yarmouth S T
BECCLES
Beccles   Beccles
1s 0½d.   FARE   1s 0½d.
THIRD CLASS
Available on day of issue only.
0024   0024

G. E. R.

Yarmouth, S.T.

102.   The grimy brickwork of the north and east walls of the concourse was covered with advertisements for all kinds of products on 2nd February 1933. (National Railway Museum)

103.   A gleaming class B12/3 4-6-0 no.8541 leaves the station with an up express in 1937. To the left of the train is the station signal box, which was destined to be demolished after suffering serious air raid damage in 1942. (G.W.Powell, courtesy R.C.Riley)

104.   The fireman checks round class D16/3 4-4-0 no.62540 as it waits to pilot a sister engine on the 2.40 pm departure on 13th March 1949. The cramped appearance and low platforms of the old station are noticeable, whilst the platform tap is well protected against any late frosts. (B.Reading)

105.   Class B17 4-6-0 no.61670 *City of London* takes water from the tank next to the turntable on 17th June 1949. This engine was one of two that had been streamlined for use on the pre-war expresses between Norwich and London, but the arrival of the B1s had relegated it to secondary duties. (B.Reading)

106. The East Suffolk line was graced with a named train when "The Easterling" was introduced in 1950. A resplendent class B1 4-6-0 no.61205 gleams in the evening sunshine as it waits to leave for London with the very first up working of this train on 5th June. (B.Reading)

107. As we look along the tracks towards the buffers in September 1950, the station has a somewhat down-at-heel appearance. The gloomy train shed is begrimed with the soot and smoke of countless arrivals, whilst the state of the right hand track and the old coach body add to the general air of neglect. Two carriage cleaners, armed with buckets and long handled brushes, are making their way along the platform. (National Railway Museum)

108. An impressive train departure board confronted passers-by on South Town Road until 1954. The absence of any information in the "Bungay & Harleston" panel suggests that the picture was taken after those two towns lost their train service in January 1953. Other long-abandoned services are recalled by panels headed "Somerleyton, Oulton Broad" (via Marsh Junction) and "Southwold Railway". (J.E.Dean)

109. On the night of 31st January 1953 the station and surrounding area suffered badly from flooding – at one time the engine shed was six feet deep in water. This was the scene a day or two later, with class B1 4-6-0 no.61054 marooned at the platform end. The Lowestoft line reopened on 4th February, but it was another 15 days before normal services via Beccles were resumed. At the time the station was undergoing a major facelift, as the building materials on the left-hand platform testify. (NRS Archive)

110. Once the floodwaters had subsided, the rebuilding work continued apace. Later in 1953 we see the framework for the new awnings taking shape on platforms 1 and 2. (B.Reading)

During the printer's strike, which delayed the closure of the Beccles-Yarmouth section, the Commercial Department had to resort to typewritten duplicated handbills.

BUFFET CAR EXCURSION

to

IPSWICH
WOODBRIDGE
SAXMUNDHAM   HALESWORTH   BECCLES
OULTON BROAD SOUTH
LOWESTOFT

and

Y A R M O U T H

SUNDAY 16th AUGUST

OUTWARD JOURNEY			RETURN JOURNEY (same day only)		
		a.m.			p.m.
Stratford	dep.	9.44	Yarmouth (South Town)	dep.	7. 0
Maryland	"	A	Lowestoft (Central)	"	7. 0
Forest Gate	"	A	Oulton Broad South	"	7. 7
Manor Park	"	A	Beccles	"	7.28
Ilford	"	A	Halesworth	"	7.42
Seven Kings	"	A	Saxmundham	"	7.59
Goodmayes	"	A	Woodbridge	"	8.16
Chadwell Heath	"	A	Ipswich	"	8.42
Romford	"	10. 4			
Gidea Park	"	B	Colchester	arr.	9.19
Harold Wood	"	B	Chelmsford	"	9.53
Brentwood	"	B	Shenfield	"	10.11
Southend-on-Sea (Victoria)	"	B	Billericay	"	B
Prittlewell	"	B	Wickford	"	B
Rochford	"	B	Rayleigh	"	B
Hockley	"	B	Hockley	"	B
Rayleigh	"	B	Rochford	"	B
Wickford	"	B	Prittlewell	"	B
Billericay	"	B	Southend-on-Sea(Victoria)	"	B
Shenfield	"	10.20	Brentwood	"	B
Chelmsford	"	10.35	Harold Wood	"	B
Colchester	"	11. 6	Gidea Park	"	B
Ipswich	"	11.38	Romford	"	10.26
Woodbridge	"	11.53	Chadwell Heath	"	A
		p.m.	Goodmayes	"	A
Saxmundham	"	12.11	Seven Kings	"	A
Halesworth	"	12.26	Ilford	"	A
Beccles	arr.	12.39	Manor Park	"	A
Oulton Broad South	"	12.59	Forest Gate	"	B
Lowestoft (Central)	"	1. 5	Maryland	"	A
Yarmouth (South Town)	"	1. 1	Stratford	"	10.41

A – By any electric train to and from Romford to connect with special train shown
B – By any electric train to and from Shenfield to connect with special train shown

FOR FARES SEE OTHER SIDE

Tickets can be obtained IN ADVANCE at stations, offices and travel agencies
Further information will be supplied on application to stations, travel agencies or to Traffic Manager, Hamilton House, Bishopsgate, London, E.C.2 (Tel:BIShopsgate 7600); District Commercial Officer, Ipswich (Tel: Ipswich 56331); or Traffic Manager, Norwich (Thorpe) (Tel: Norwich 20371)

CONDITIONS OF ISSUE

London, July 1959
PP/51/16

111.　After two years work, the improvements were completed in July 1954 and provided modern facilities for staff and passengers alike, whilst the brickwork received a thorough cleaning. The local newspaper reported "The general impression is of brightness and cleanliness", and their photograph of the finished product on 14th July 1954 illustrates this perfectly. (Eastern Counties Newspapers)

112.　Class F5 2-4-2T no. 67199 heads a train for Lowestoft away from the station on 9th October 1956. It is passing the rather austere looking signal box which had replaced its bomb-damaged predecessor some 13 years earlier. (R.C.Riley)

113.　A Metro Cammell DMU stands in platform 3 on 30th July 1958, flanked by a class N7 0-6-2T shunting coaches in the sidings and a gas tank wagon on the centre road. The clean concrete platforms, smart awnings and electric lighting provide a dramatic contrast with the old station. (Frank Church courtesy E.B.E.G.)

114. "Sandringham" class 4-6-0 no.61664 *Liverpool* is signalled out of platform 1 on the same day, as a Derby Lightweight DMU approaches platform 3. It is difficult to believe that this busy railway scene would be reduced to just a single track within ten years.
(Frank Church courtesy E.B.E.G.)

115. The blue and white containers carrying Birds Eye frozen foods from their factory at Yarmouth were a colourful but short-lived feature of the railway scene during the late 1950s and early 1960s. One of the 4-ton insulated containers stands in the goods yard on 9th June 1959. The run-down of freight facilities in the mid-1960s was gradual, complete closure taking place on 6th November 1967. (R.J.Adderson)

116. After years of neglect, the engine shed was rebuilt in the late 1950s. This is the south end of the shed on 18th July 1959, with an ex GER 0-6-0T at the buffer stops and a class L1 2-6-4T simmering as it awaits its next duty. (G.L.Kenworthy collection)

117.   Despite the closure of the Beccles line, the station still looks prosperous enough as a two car Metro Cammell DMU forms the 10.30 am train for Ipswich on 20th September 1963. The rot has set in though, as a dark patch between the seats on the concourse reveals that the bookstall had been removed. One of the station seats, with a crab cast into the end support, can be seen at the National Railway Museum at York. (R.J.Adderson)

118.   In its final years the Lowestoft line was just a single track, making its forlorn way through the acres of derelict railway land to the vandalised and neglected station. This picture, taken from the signal box steps on the last day of operation, sums up those final sad days. (R.J.Adderson)

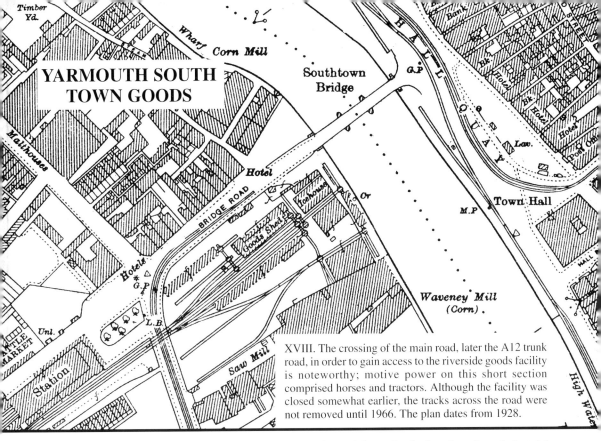

YARMOUTH SOUTH TOWN GOODS

XVIII. The crossing of the main road, later the A12 trunk road, in order to gain access to the riverside goods facility is noteworthy; motive power on this short section comprised horses and tractors. Although the facility was closed somewhat earlier, the tracks across the road were not removed until 1966. The plan dates from 1928.

119. The yard to the north of the road served a substantial goods shed and various industrial premises. Here we see a typical shunting operation during the early years of the twentieth century, with the goods shed in the background and one of the wagon turntables to the left. This was one of a dozen that enabled the railway to make maximum use of the rather cramped site. (M.King Collection)

120.   Here is the exterior of the station building as it was on 2nd February 1933, with the tracks serving the riverside goods yard in the foreground. As late as the 1960s, town centre traffic was occasionally brought to a standstill as a tractor propelled a wagon across the busy main road on its way to or from the yard. (National Railway Museum)

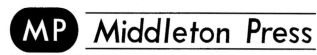

MP Middleton Press

Easebourne Lane, Midhurst, W Sussex. GU29 9AZ Tel: 01730 813169 Fax: 01730 812601
Email: sales@middletonpress.co.uk www.middletonpress.co.uk
If books are not available from your local transport stockist, order direct post free UK.

BRANCH LINES
Branch Line to Allhallows
Branch Line to Alton
Branch Lines around Ascot
Branch Line to Ashburton
Branch Lines around Bodmin
Branch Line to Bude
Branch Lines around Canterbury
Branch Lines around Chard & Yeovil
Branch Line to Cheddar
Branch Lines around Cromer
Branch Line to the Derwent Valley
Branch Lines to East Grinstead
Branch Lines of East London
Branch Lines to Effingham Junction
Branch Lines to Falmouth, Helston & St. Ives
Branch Lines to Fairford
Branch Lines to Felixstowe & Aldeburgh
Branch Lines around Gosport
Branch Line to Hayling
Branch Lines to Henley, Windsor & Marlow
Branch Line to Hawkhurst
Branch Line to Horsham
Branch Lines around Huntingdon
Branch Line to Ilfracombe
Branch Line to Kingsbridge
Branch Line to Kingswear
Branch Line to Lambourn
Branch Lines to Launceston & Princetown
Branch Line to Longmoor
Branch Line to Looe
Branch Line to Lyme Regis
Branch Line to Lynton
Branch Lines around March
Branch Lines around Midhurst
Branch Line to Minehead
Branch Line to Moretonhampstead
Branch Lines to Newport (IOW)
Branch Lines to Newquay
Branch Lines around North Woolwich
Branch Line to Padstow
Branch Lines to Princes Risborough
Branch Lines to Seaton and Sidmouth
Branch Lines around Sheerness
Branch Line to Shrewsbury
Branch Line to Tenterden
Branch Lines around Tiverton
Branch Lines to Torrington
Branch Lines to Tunbridge Wells
Branch Line to Upwell
Branch Line to Wantage (The Wantage Tramway)
Branch Lines of West London
Branch Lines of West Wiltshire
Branch Lines around Weymouth
Branch Lines around Wimborne
Branch Lines around Wisbech

NARROW GAUGE
Austrian Narrow Gauge
Branch Line to Lynton
Branch Lines around Portmadoc 1923-46
Branch Lines around Porthmadog 1954-94
Branch Line to Southwold
Douglas to Port Erin
Douglas to Peel
Kent Narrow Gauge
Northern France Narrow Gauge
Romneyrail
Sierra Leone Narrow Gauge
Southern France Narrow Gauge
Sussex Narrow Gauge
Surrey Narrow Gauge

Swiss Narrow Gauge
Two-Foot Gauge Survivors
Vivarais Narrow Gauge

SOUTH COAST RAILWAYS
Ashford to Dover
Bournemouth to Weymouth
Brighton to Worthing
Dover to Ramsgate
Eastbourne to Hastings
Hastings to Ashford
Portsmouth to Southampton
Ryde to Ventnor
Southampton to Bournemouth

SOUTHERN MAIN LINES
Basingstoke to Salisbury
Crawley to Littlehampton
Dartford to Sittingbourne
East Croydon to Three Bridges
Epsom to Horsham
Exeter to Barnstaple
Exeter to Tavistock
London Bridge to East Croydon
Orpington to Tonbridge
Tonbridge to Hastings
Salisbury to Yeovil
Sittingbourne to Ramsgate
Swanley to Ashford
Tavistock to Plymouth
Three Bridges to Brighton
Victoria to Bromley South
Victoria to East Croydon
Waterloo to Windsor
Waterloo to Woking
Woking to Portsmouth
Woking to Southampton
Yeovil to Exeter

EASTERN MAIN LINES
Barking to Southend
Ely to Kings Lynn
Ely to Norwich
Fenchurch Street to Barking
Hitchin to Peterborough
Ilford to Shenfield
Ipswich to Saxmundham
Liverpool Street to Ilford
Saxmundham to Yarmouth
Tilbury Loop

WESTERN MAIN LINES
Banbury to Birmingham
Bristol to Taunton
Didcot to Banbury
Didcot to Swindon
Ealing to Slough
Exeter to Newton Abbot
Moreton-in-Marsh to Worcester
Newton Abbot to Plymouth
Newbury to Westbury
Oxford to Moreton-in-Marsh
Paddington to Ealing
Paddington to Princes Risborough
Plymouth to St. Austell
Princes Risborough to Banbury
Reading to Didcot
Slough to Newbury
St. Austell to Penzance
Swindon to Bristol
Swindon to Newport
Taunton to Exeter
Westbury to Taunton

MIDLAND MAIN LINES
St. Albans to Bedford
Euston to Harrow & Wealdstone
Harrow to Watford
St. Pancras to St. Albans

COUNTRY RAILWAY ROUTES
Abergavenny to Merthyr
Andover to Southampton
Bath to Evercreech Junction
Bath Green Park to Bristol
Bournemouth to Evercreech Junction
Brecon to Newport
Burnham to Evercreech Junction
Cheltenham to Andover
Croydon to East Grinstead
Didcot to Winchester
East Kent Light Railway
Frome to Bristol
Guildford to Redhill
Reading to Basingstoke
Reading to Guildford
Redhill to Ashford
Salisbury to Westbury
Stratford upon Avon to Cheltenham
Strood to Paddock Wood
Taunton to Barnstaple
Wenford Bridge to Fowey
Westbury to Bath
Woking to Alton
Yeovil to Dorchester

GREAT RAILWAY ERAS
Ashford from Steam to Eurostar
Clapham Junction 50 years of change
Festiniog in the Fifties
Festiniog in the Sixties
Festiniog 50 years of enterprise
Isle of Wight Lines 50 years of change
Railways to Victory 1944-46
Return to Blaenau 1970-82
SECR Centenary album
Talyllyn 50 years of change
Wareham to Swanage 50 years of change
Yeovil 50 years of change

LONDON SUBURBAN RAILWAYS
Caterham and Tattenham Corner
Charing Cross to Dartford
Clapham Jn. to Beckenham Jn.
Crystal Palace (HL) & Catford Loop
East London Line
Finsbury Park to Alexandra Palace
Holborn Viaduct to Lewisham
Kingston and Hounslow Loops
Lewisham to Dartford
Liverpool Street to Chingford
Mitcham Junction Lines
North London Line
South London Line
West Croydon to Epsom
West London Line
Willesden Junction to Richmond
Wimbledon to Beckenham
Wimbledon to Epsom

STEAMING THROUGH
Steaming through Cornwall
Steaming through the Isle of Wight
Steaming through Kent
Steaming through West Hants

TRAMWAY CLASSICS
Aldgate & Stepney Tramways
Barnet & Finchley Tramways
Bath Tramways
Brighton's Tramways
Bristol's Tramways
Burton & Ashby Tramways
Camberwell & W.Norwood Tramways
Clapham & Streatham Tramways
Croydon's Tramways
Derby Tramways
Dover's Tramways
East Ham & West Ham Tramways
Edgware and Willesden Tramways
Eltham & Woolwich Tramways
Embankment & Waterloo Tramways
Exeter & Taunton Tramways
Fulwell - Home to Trams, Trolleys and Buses
Great Yarmouth Tramways
Greenwich & Dartford Tramways
Hammersmith & Hounslow Tramways
Hampstead & Highgate Tramways
Hastings Tramways
Holborn & Finsbury Tramways
Ilford & Barking Tramways
Kingston & Wimbledon Tramways
Lewisham & Catford Tramways
Liverpool Tramways 1. Eastern Routes
Liverpool Tramways 2. Southern Routes
Liverpool Tramways 3. Northern Routes
Maidstone & Chatham Tramways
Margate to Ramsgate
North Kent Tramways
Norwich Tramways
Reading Tramways
Shepherds Bush & Uxbridge Tramways
Southend-on-sea Tramways
South London Line Tramways 1903-33
Southwark & Deptford Tramways
Stamford Hill Tramways
Twickenham & Kingston Tramways
Victoria & Lambeth Tramways
Waltham Cross & Edmonton Tramways
Walthamstow & Leyton Tramways
Wandsworth & Battersea Tramways

TROLLEYBUS CLASSICS
Bradford Trolleybuses
Croydon Trolleybuses
Derby Trolleybuses
Hastings Trolleybuses
Huddersfield Trolleybuses
Hull Trolleybuses
Maidstone Trolleybuses
Portsmouth Trolleybuses
Reading Trolleybuses

WATERWAY & SHIPPING
Kent and East Sussex Waterways
London to Portsmouth Waterway
Sussex Shipping - Sail, Steam & Motor
West Sussex Waterways

MILITARY BOOKS
Battle over Portsmouth
Battle over Sussex 1940
Blitz over Sussex 1941-42
Bombers over Sussex 1943-45
Bognor at War
East Ridings Secret Resistance
Military Defence of West Sussex
Military Signals from the South Coast
Secret Sussex Resistance
Surrey Home Guard

OTHER RAILWAY BOOKS
Industrial Railways of the South-East
South Eastern & Chatham Railways
London Chatham & Dover Railway
London Termini - Past and Proposed
War on the Line (SR 1939-45)